What are penguins?

A penguin can swim through the water just like a fish.

Penguins are birds. But penguins cannot fly. They like to swim instead. There are 17 **species** of penguin in the world.

species different types of an animal that all share the same name.

ANIMALS A M A Z I N G

PENGUINS

BY VALERIE BODDEN

W
FRANKLIN WATTS
LONDON•SYDNEY

This edition 2013

First published in the UK in 2012 by
Franklin Watts
338 Euston Road
London NW1 3BH

Franklin Watts Australia
Level 17/207 Kent Street
Sydney NSW 2000

First published by Creative Education,
an imprint of the Creative Company.
Copyright © 2010 Creative Education
International copyright reserved in all countries.
No part of this book may be reproduced in any
form without written permission from the publisher.

All rights reserved.

ISBN 978 1 4451 2735 4
Dewey number: 598.4'7

A CIP catalogue record for this book
is available from the British Library.

Printed in China

Franklin Watts is a division of
Hachette Children's Books
an Hachette UK company
www.hachette.co.uk

Book and cover design by The Design Lab
Art direction by Rita Marshall

Photographs by Getty Images (Ira Block, Bill
Curtsinger, Tui De Roy, John Eastcott and Yva
Momatiuk, Darrell Gulin, Johnny Johnson, Ty Milford,
Paul Nicklen, Flip Nicklin, Joseph Van Os, Norbert
Wu), iStockphoto (Sam Lee, Jan Will)

CONTENTS

Penguin facts

Most penguins have long, fat bodies and very short legs. They are covered with feathers. Penguins have dark feathers on their backs and light feathers on their bellies. Some types of penguin have yellow or orange feathers on their head. Male and female penguins look alike. It is very hard to tell them apart. Penguins have a small tail and short, stiff wings called flippers.

Dark feathers help penguins to absorb the Sun's heat. This helps them to keep warm.

Big and small penguins

Penguins come in many different sizes. Little blue penguins are the smallest penguins. They are only 40 centimetres tall. They weigh about 1.5 kilogrammes. This is less than a new human baby. Emperor penguins are the biggest penguins. They can be over a metre tall and weigh up to 40 kilogrammes!

This rockhopper penguin is a small-sized penguin.

Where penguins live

All wild penguins live near the sea in the Southern Hemisphere (*HEM-is-feer*). Many penguins live in the continent of Antarctica. It is very cold there and the land is covered with ice. Other penguins live in the continents of South America, Australia, and Africa.

Penguins like to dive off the icy land into the sea.

Hemisphere one of the two halves of the Earth. There is one in the north and one in the south.
continent one of Earth's seven big pieces of land.

Penguin food

Adult penguins share food with their chicks.

Penguins eat food from the ocean. Most penguins eat small fish such as anchovies (*AN-cho-vees*) or sardines. Other penguins eat **krill**. Some penguins eat squid. Penguins need to eat a lot of food every day. The extra food is turned into fat. This helps the penguins to stay warm in the cold water.

krill tiny water animals that look like prawns.

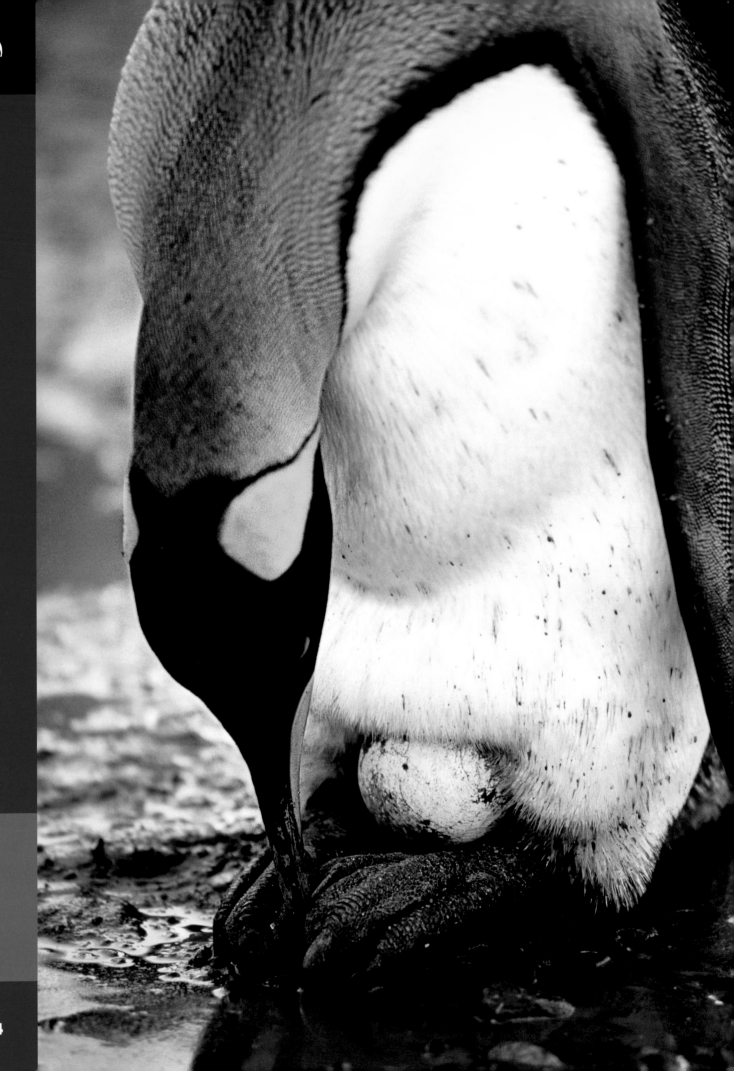

New penguins

*Mother and father penguins
take good care of their eggs.*

Mother penguins lay one or two eggs at a time. Mother and father penguins take turns caring for the eggs. A **chick** will hatch out of each egg. Chicks are covered with **down**. When the chicks have grown their adult feathers, they are old enough to look after themselves. Wild penguins can live for 15 to 20 years.

chick a baby penguin.
down the warm, soft and fluffy feathers on a baby bird.

Penguins underwater

Penguins like to swim in groups with other penguins.

Penguins are very good at swimming. They spend a lot of time underwater looking for food. They flap their flippers to move through the water. Their feathers are **waterproof**. This helps them to stay warm and dry. Some penguins stay in the water for many months at a time.

waterproof able to stop water from getting in.

Penguins on land

There can be thousands of penguins in some colonies.

When penguins are on land, they gather in a big group called a **colony**. They stay together to keep warm. The groups are noisy! Penguins can honk, squawk and **bray**.

colony a large group.
bray a sound like a donkey can make.

Penguins and people

Penguins can slide faster than they can walk!

Most people do not live near penguins. But lots of people like to watch penguins in zoos. It is fun to watch them swim through the water. Some people even go to the Antarctic to see penguins in the wild. They can watch them slide over the ice on their bellies. This is called **tobogganing**!

tobogganing sliding over snow or ice. When people toboggan we sometimes call it 'sledging'.

A *penguin story*

Why are emperor penguins so big? People on the continent of South America tell a story about this. They say that once there was a flood. Water covered the whole world. People had to live in the water. Some of them climbed onto big sheets of ice to live with the penguins. After a while, the people turned into penguins.

They became the biggest penguins of all – emperor penguins!

Useful information

Read More

Really Weird Animals: Birds by Clare Hibbert (Franklin Watts, 2011)

Watery Worlds: Polar Seas by Jinny Johnson (Franklin Watts, 2012)

Michaela Strachan's Really Wild Adventures: A book of fun and factual animal rhymes by Michaela Strachan (Franklin Watts, 2012)

Websites

http://gowild.wwf.org.uk/regions/polar-fact-files/adelie-penguin
This site has lots of facts about adelie penguins and fun activities on all things polar.

http://kids.nationalgeographic.com/kids/animals/creaturefeature/emperor-penguin/
This site is all about the emperor penguin. Click on the penguin picture in the 'select another creature' section to find out about other types of penguin.

http://www.kidzone.ws/animals/penguins
This site has great penguin facts, activities, and photos.

Every effort has been made by the Publishers to ensure that these websites are suitable for children, that they are of the highest educational value and that they contain no inappropriate or offensive material. However, because of the nature of the Internet, it is impossible to guarantee that the contents of these sites will not be altered. We strongly advise that Internet access is supervised by a responsible adult.

Index